SCENE BY SCENE
COMPARATIVE WORKBOOK HL17

The Fault in Our Stars

by John Green

Theme/Issue - Relationships

Literary Genre

General Vision and Viewpoint

Copyright © 2016 by Amy Farrell.

All rights reserved. No part of this publication may be reproduced, distributed or transmitted in any form or by any means, including photocopying, recording, or other electronic or mechanical methods, without the prior written permission of the publisher, except in the case of brief quotations embodied in critical reviews and certain other noncommercial uses permitted by copyright law. For permission requests, write to the publisher, addressed "Attention: Permissions Coordinator," at the address below.

Scene by Scene
11 Millfield, Enniskerry
Wicklow, Ireland.
www.scenebysceneguides.com

info@scenebysceneguides.com

The Fault in Our Stars Comparative Workbook HL17 by Amy Farrell. —1st ed.
ISBN 978-1-910949-42-9

The Fault in Our Stars Comparative Study Workbook

This workbook is designed to help Leaving Certificate English students become familiar with the Comparative Study modes and to understand how each mode may be applied to *The Fault in Our Stars*.

The Comparative Study Modes at Higher Level for 2017 are:

Theme/Issue

The theme covered in this workbook is Relationships. This theme can be applied to any relationship in a text and covers love, marriage, friendship and family bonds.

Consider the complexities of relationships and the impact they have on characters' lives.

Literary Genre

This mode refers to the way the story is told.

Consider aspects of narration such as the manner and style of narration, characterisation, setting, tension, literary techniques, etc.

The General Vision and Viewpoint

This mode refers to the author's outlook or view of life and how this viewpoint is represented in the text.

Consider whether the text is bright or dark, optimistic or pessimistic, uplifting or bleak, etc.

How Does it Work?

This workbook has three parts, one each for Theme/Issue (our chosen theme for study is Relationships), Literary Genre and General Vision and Viewpoint. Each part has three sections: Know the Text, Know the Mode and Compare the Texts.

Know The Text

These questions are on *The Fault in Our Stars* text and refer specifically to this novel. Through answering these questions you will get to know the text well, while also getting a feel for the Comparative Study mode the questions relate to.

Know the Mode

These questions use 'mode' specific terms and phrases and are intended to help prepare you for tackling exam questions. They focus on the mode itself, rather than the text you have studied. You apply your knowledge of the text to the mode in question.

Compare the Texts

These questions ask you to compare your texts under specific aspects of each mode. It is important that you get used to the idea of comparing and contrasting your chosen texts, as this is what the Comparative Study is all about. It is good practice to think about your texts in terms of their similarities and differences within each mode.

This approach is designed to prevent 'drift' between modes and focuses on analysis and personal response, rather than summary.

Theme/Issue - Know the Text

1 Are Hazel's parents good parents? Do they strive to have a loving relationship with her? Is theirs a loving family? Why/ why not?

2 Is Hazel a good daughter?
Does she love, respect and understand her parents?

THE FAULT IN OUR STARS - THEME/ISSUE - RELATIONSHIPS

3 How well do Hazel and her parents **communicate**, interact and understand one another?

4 What makes it difficult for Hazel's parents to parent her?

KNOW THE TEXT

5 Does Hazel's relationship with her parents **change** during the course of the novel?

6 What **strengths** do you see in Hazel's relationship with her parents?

THE FAULT IN OUR STARS - THEME/ISSUE - RELATIONSHIPS

7 What **weaknesses** or problems do you see in Hazel's relationship with her parents?

8 Is this a positive or negative relationship? Use examples to justify your view.

9 In what ways is Hazel's relationship with her parents similar to that of Augustus and his parents? Can you explain these similarities?

10 Is Augustus a good match for Hazel?

THE FAULT IN OUR STARS - THEME/ISSUE - RELATIONSHIPS

11 Do Hazel and Augustus have a normal teenage relationship? Explain your view.

12 How well do Hazel and Augustus **communicate**, interact and understand one another?

KNOW THE TEXT

13 What causes problems in this relationship?

14 What made Hazel distance herself from Augustus in the first half of the novel? How did it affect their relationship? Do you understand why she did this?

15 Does Hazel's relationship with Augustus **change** during the course of the novel? Explain.

16 What **strengths** do you see in Hazel's relationship with Augustus?

KNOW THE TEXT

17 What **weaknesses** or problems do you see in Hazel's relationship with Augustus?

18 Is this a positive or negative relationship?

THE FAULT IN OUR STARS - THEME/ISSUE - RELATIONSHIPS

19 Does anything sadden you about Hazel's relationship with Augustus?

20 Does being together make Hazel and Augustus happy?

KNOW THE TEXT

21 Do Hazel and Augustus love one another?

22 What does their relationship teach us about love?

THE FAULT IN OUR STARS - THEME/ISSUE - RELATIONSHIPS

23 Comment on Isaac's relationship with his girlfriend.

24 Comment on Augustus' friendship with Isaac.

Theme/Issue - Know the Mode

25 Are relationships in this text generally **positive** (warm, supportive, nurturing, genuine) or **negative** (cold, cruel, destructive, false)?

THE FAULT IN OUR STARS - THEME/ISSUE - RELATIONSHIPS

26 What makes relationships in this text complicated and **difficult**?

27 What would **improve** relationships in this text?

28 How do relationships **change** during the story?

KNOW THE MODE

29 What did **you learn** about relationships from reading this novel?

THE FAULT IN OUR STARS - THEME/ISSUE - RELATIONSHIPS

30 Are relationships **portrayed realistically** in this text? Make use of examples to support the points you make.

KNOW THE MODE

31 Are relationships in this story **interesting** and **involving**?

32 Did anything about the theme of relationships in this text **shock, upset** or **unsettle** you?

KNOW THE MODE

33 What is the **most signficant relationship** in this text?
What makes it so significant and important?

34 Do relationships in this story bring characters **happiness** or **sorrow**?

KNOW THE MODE

35 Choose **key moments** from this story that highlight relationships in the text.

Theme/Issue - Compare the Texts

36 Were relationships in *The Fault in Our Stars* more positive and supportive than the relationships in your other texts? Give specific examples.

37 Rank the relationships you have studied in your various texts from most positive to most negative. Add a note to explain your choices.

38

Were relationships in *The Fault in Our Stars* the most engaging and interesting that you have studied? Explain your choice.

39 Rank the relationships you have studied in your various texts from most interesting to least interesting. Add a note to explain your choices.

40 Did you **learn most** about the theme of relationships from this text or another text on your comparative course?

41 What **similarities** do you notice in the theme of relationships in this text and your other comparative texts?

COMPARE THE TEXTS

42 What **differences** do you notice in the theme of relationships in this text and your other comparative texts?

COMPARE THE TEXTS

THE FAULT IN OUR STARS - LITERARY GENRE

Literary Genre - Know the Text

43 How is this story told? (Consider the novel format).

44 Why is the story told in this way?
What is the effect of this?

> **45** Is Hazel a good choice of **narrator**? Explain your view.

> **46** How does Green develop Hazel's character?

THE FAULT IN OUR STARS - LITERARY GENRE

47 Were you captivated by this story? Did you find yourself wanting to read on, or was it a chore? Give reasons for your answer.

48 Did you like Hazel and Augustus? Were they interesting lead characters? Explain your choice.

> **49** Does **Amsterdam symbolise** or represent anything for Hazel and Augustus?

> **50** Does the teenagers' date at Oranjee have a significant or deeper meaning?

51 How do you respond to the **love story** aspect of this text?

52 Augustus falls ill in Chapter 13. Why did John Green tell us of his illness at this point? How does this add to the emotional impact of the story? What issues does Green want us to consider?

53 Is Augustus' illness an **unexpected twist**? What hints, if any, are there that Augustus was unwell? Does this knowledge prepare us adequately for his death?
How does it add to the story?

54 What role does Van Houten play in the novel?

55 What role does Isaac play in the novel?

56 What role does illness and cancer play in the story?

KNOW THE TEXT

57 Is this a novel about death, grief, love or something else?

58 Did you feel you got to know the characters in this story well? Why/why not?

59 *The Fault in Our Stars* has been a 'smash hit' with Young Adult readers around the world.
Why is this the case, in your opinion?

Literary Genre - Know the Mode

60 Did **you** enjoy the **storyline** of the text?
Was it exciting/compelling/tense/emotional?
Why/why not?

61 Is there just one **plot** or many plots?
What connections can you make between the storylines?

62 What three things interested **you** most in the story?

KNOW THE MODE

63 Are **characters** vivid, realistic and well-developed?

64 Do **you** empathise or **identify** with any character(s)?
Did you become involved in this story or care about the characters? Use examples.

65 Who was your **favourite character**?
What aspects of this character did you enjoy?

66 Consider Hazel as the novel's **heroine**. What made Hazel a **memorable** or **interesting** character?

67 Who was your **least favourite character**? What aspects of this character did you dislike? What made them a memorable or interesting character?

68 Is the story humorous or tragic, romantic or realistic? Explain using examples.

69 To what **genre** does it belong?
What aspects of this genre did **you** enjoy?
Is it Romance, Thriller, Horror, Action/Adventure, Historical, Fantasy, Science-fiction, Satire, etc.?

THE FAULT IN OUR STARS - LITERARY GENRE

70 How does the author create **suspense**, **high emotion** and **excitement** in the text? What **techniques** does he use to good advantage?

71 Consider the author's use of **tension** and **resolution** in the novel. What are the major **tensions/problems/conflicts** in the text? Are they **resolved** or not?

72 Did the author make use of any striking patterns of **imagery** or **symbols** to add to the story?

73 How does the author make use of the **unexpected** in this text? What did this add to the story? (Think about key moments here.)

KNOW THE MODE

74 What is the **climax** (high point) of the story?

75 What did **you** think of this moment?
How did it make **you feel**?

THE FAULT IN OUR STARS – LITERARY GENRE

76 Comment on the **language** of the novel. How does dialogue add to the story?

77 Comment on the **pacing** of the novel. How does this add to the story?

78 Comment on the **setting** of the novel. Consider time, place, and specific locations such as Amsterdam. How does setting add to your understanding of the characters and their story?

79 Was anything about this novel **moving** or **emotional**?
Think of moments in the novel that you responded to. What made them moving? How did this add to the story?

80 On a scale of one to ten, how much did you enjoy the **ending**? What was satisfying/unsatisfying about it? Was anything left unanswered?

81 The experiences of seeing a play, reading a novel and viewing a film are very different.
What aspects of the **novel form** worked well in this story, in your opinion?

82 What did **you** like about **the way** the story was told?
*Mention aspects of storytelling and literary techniques that **you** found enjoyable. Refer to key moments.*

83 Identify **key moments** in the novel that illustrate Literary Genre (the way the story is told). Clearly **define literary techniques/aspects of narrative** in your analysis.

KNOW THE MODE

Literary Genre - Compare the Texts

84 Did **you** like the way this story was told more than your other comparative texts?
State what you enjoyed most about each.

85 Is *The Fault in Our Stars* more **exciting** than your other texts?
Consider tension, pacing, suspense, conflict and the unexpected.

86 Are **characters** more engaging in this novel than in your other texts?
Refer to each of your texts in your answer.

87 Is the **setting** more effective in telling this story than in your other texts?
Refer to each of your texts in your answer.

88 Is this story more **unpredictable** than your other texts?
Refer to each of your texts in your answer.

89 Did this novel have greater **emotional power** than your other texts?
Was emotional power created in a more interesting way here or in a different text?

90 What **similarities** do you notice in the Literary Genre of this novel and your other comparative texts?
Mention specific aspects of narrative.

COMPARE THE TEXTS

91 What **differences** do you notice in the Literary Genre of this novel and your other comparative texts?
Mention specific aspects of narrative.

COMPARE THE TEXTS

General Vision and Viewpoint - Know the Text

92 Do Hazel and Augustus love and support one another? Is their relationship a positive or negative comment on life?

93 How does Hazel's illness impact on the General Vision and Viewpoint of the text?
Does her illness brighten or darken the mood of the text? How does it impact on her family? How does it impact on her future?

KNOW THE TEXT

94 Why is Hazel afraid to pursue a relationship with Augustus at first? How does her reluctance impact on the atmosphere and mood of the story?

95 What makes Hazel change her mind about pursuing a relationship with Augustus? How do her actions here impact on the mood and atmosphere of the story?

| 96 | How does the trip to Amsterdam to meet Van Houten impact on the mood and atmosphere of the text? |

| 97 | What does Hazel and Augustus' love story suggest about life? |

KNOW THE TEXT

98 How does Augustus' death affect the mood of the story?
What does his death suggest about life?

99 Death is a theme of this novel.
Does this mean it has a morbid outlook?

THE FAULT IN OUR STARS - GENERAL VISION AND VIEWPOINT

100 Does this text tell us anything about **suffering** and the **human spirit**? Explain your view.

101 Does this text tell us anything about **love**?

KNOW THE TEXT

102 How does Isaac's illness and blindness contribute to the mood of the story?

103 How does the closing section make you feel?
Use 'I' statements to develop your Personal Response.

104	Is Hazel's future promising? Will she be happy in life, do you think?

105	What lessons about life have you learned by the novel's ending? Did you find this text to be uplifting or saddening? Explain your view.

106

"The world is not a wish-granting factory."
How does this line contribute to John Green's General Vision and Viewpoint?
If it is not a wish-granting factory, then what is it?

107

What is John Green telling us about life in this story?
What is John Green's message?
Is his outlook positive or negative, in your view?

General Vision and Viewpoint - Know the Mode

108 Identify bright/hopeful/optimistic aspects of the novel.

109 Identify dark/hopeless/pessimistic aspects of the novel.

110
Is this text **optimistic** or **pessimistic**? Explain. *Consider characters' happiness, imagery, atmosphere, future prospects, etc.*

111
On a scale of one to ten, how optimistic is this text?

KNOW THE MODE

112 Identify the **aspects of life** that the author concentrates on.
Are they positive or negative?
Consider overcoming adversity, illness, bravery, suffering, love, etc.

THE FAULT IN OUR STARS – GENERAL VISION AND VIEWPOINT

> **113** What **comments** do characters make on their **society** and the problems they're facing?

KNOW THE MODE

114 Are characters happy or unhappy?

115 What makes characters in this story happy and fulfilled?

THE FAULT IN OUR STARS - GENERAL VISION AND VIEWPOINT

116 What makes characters in this story unhappy and unfulfilled?

117 Are **relationships** destructive or nurturing? What do they reveal about life, as we see characters supported/thwarted in their efforts to grow/mature?

118 Are **imagery** and **language** bright or dark in the text? (Tone of the text)

119 What is the **mood** of this text?

120 What does this story **teach us about life?**
What do we learn about life's hardships? Are struggles overcome? Is determination rewarded? Is life difficult or joyful?

121 How do you **feel** as you read this novel?
Refer to key moments to anchor your answer.

122 How do you **feel** at the **end**?

123
Are questions raised by the text **resolved** by the end?
Are they resolved **happily** or **unhappily**?

124 Are **you hopeful** or **despairing** regarding the prospects for human **happiness** in this story?
Are characters likely to be happy?

125 Identify the **key moments** in the novel that illustrate the General Vision and Viewpoint of the text.

KNOW THE MODE

General Vision and Viewpoint - Compare the Texts

126 Is life happier for characters in this story than in your other comparative texts? Explain.

127

Do characters in this text face more obstacles and difficulties than in your other texts?
Who struggles most?

128 Are characters in this text **rewarded more** for their struggles than in your other texts?
By overcoming adversity, do they achieve true happiness and contentment in a way that is not realised in your other texts?

COMPARE THE TEXTS

129 Is this the brightest, most hopeful and triumphant text you have studied? Explain why its message is more or less positive than your other texts.

130 Which of your chosen texts was the bleakest and most upsetting or depressing?
Explain why it was more negative than your other texts. What made them more positive?

131

Plot your three texts on a scale of one to ten, from darkest (most pessimistic) to brightest (most optimistic). Add points to explain their position.

132 What **similarities** do you notice in the General Vision and Viewpoint of this text and your other comparative texts?

COMPARE THE TEXTS

133 What **differences** do you notice in the General Vision and Viewpoint of this text and your other comparative texts?

COMPARE THE TEXTS

www.ingramcontent.com/pod-product-compliance
Lightning Source LLC
Chambersburg PA
CBHW050714090526
44587CB00019B/3373